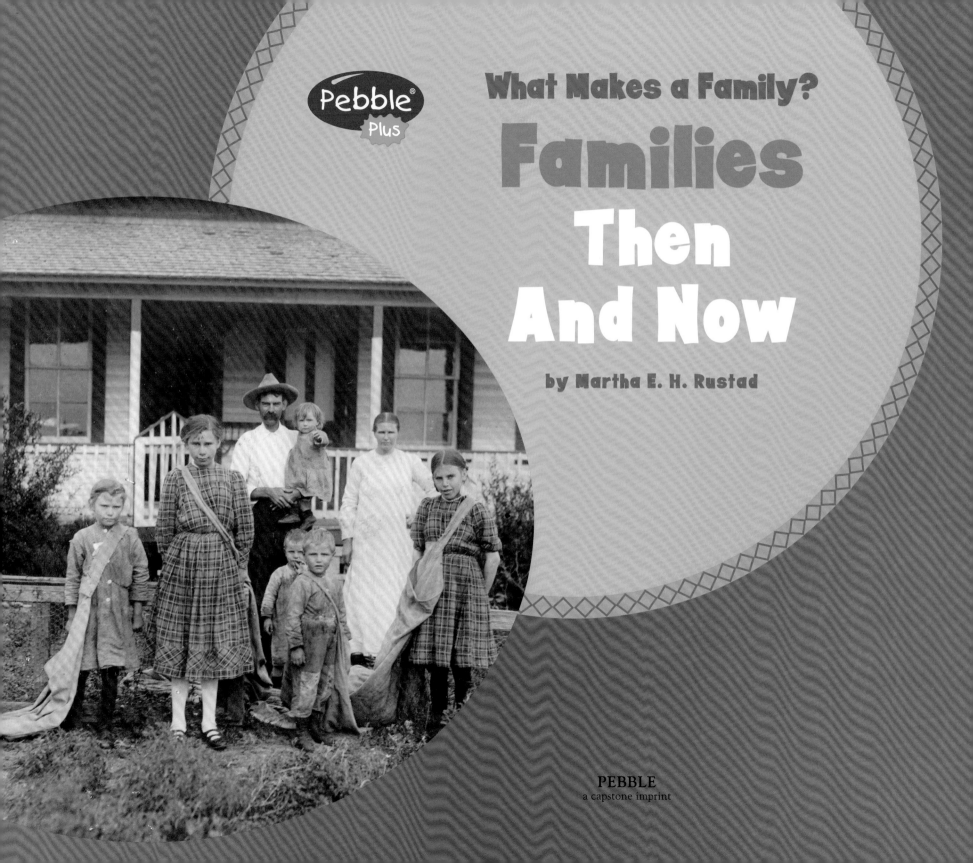

Pebble® Plus

What Makes a Family?

Families
Then
And Now

by Martha E. H. Rustad

PEBBLE
a capstone imprint

Pebble Plus is published by Pebble
1710 Roe Crest Drive,
North Mankato, Minnesota 56003
www.mycapstone.com

Library of Congress Cataloging-in-Publication Data
Library of Congress Cataloging-in-Publication Data is available on the Library of Congress website.
ISBN 978-1-9771-0903-3 (library binding)
ISBN 978-1-9771-1051-0 (paperback)
ISBN 978-1-9771-1273-6 (eBook PDF)

Editorial Credits
Marissa Kirkman, editor; Cynthia Della-Rovere, designer;
Eric Gohl, media researcher; Tori Abraham, production specialist

Image Credits
Library of Congress: 1, 7, 9, 13, 15, 21; Shutterstock: Africa Studio, 19, Creativa Images, 17, Cultura Motion, cover,
Monkey Business Images, 5, 11
Design Elements: Shutterstock

All internet sites appearing in back matter were available and accurate when this book was sent to press.

Note to Parents and Teachers
The What Makes a Family? set supports national standards related to social studies. This book describes and illustrates
how families have changed over the years. The images support early readers in understanding the text. The repetition
of words and phrases helps early readers learn new words. This book also introduces early readers to subject-specific
vocabulary words, which are defined in the Glossary section. Early readers may need assistance to read some words
and to use the Table of Contents, Glossary, Read More, Internet Sites, Critical Thinking Questions, and Index sections of
the book.

Printed and bound in China.
001654

Table of Contents

Then and Now

Here is a family today.

Adults and kids share a home.

Sometimes pets join the family

too. Families share lots of love.

This is a family from long ago.

They shared this home.

How are the families

from then and now alike?

How are they different?

Homes

Long ago, many families had
lots of kids. Many families lived
on farms. Kids helped on
the farm by doing chores.
They still had time to play.

9

Today, most families have only
a few kids. Not as many families
live on farms today. But kids
still do chores in their homes.
And they still find time to play.

Long ago, some families lived in cities. They lived in apartments or houses. Today, many families still live in cities. Some families live outside of cities, in suburbs or in the country.

Going Places

Long ago, families traveled by horse and wagon. A family trip was a visit to the store in town. It took all day to travel to town and back home.

Today, families travel by cars, buses, or airplanes. Many families take trips. They can travel far from home in a few hours. They visit family and friends.

Keeping in Touch

Long ago, kids wrote letters
by hand. It took days or weeks
to deliver them in the mail.
Today, kids can call and text
on the phone.

Long ago, families spent time together. They showed their love. Today, families still spend time together. They show their love for each other in new ways.

Glossary

apartment—a home that has its own rooms and front door, but shares outside walls and a roof with other apartments

chore—a job that has to be done regularly; washing dishes and taking out the garbage are chores

deliver—to take something to a place or a person

store—a place where things are sold

suburb—a town or village near a city

wagon—a vehicle with wheels that is used to carry heavy loads; horses pull some wagons.

Read More

Dinmont, Kerry. *Homes Past and Present*. Past and Present. Minneapolis: Lerner Publications, 2019.

Lewis, Clare. *Home Life Through the Years*. History in Living Memory. Chicago: Heinemann Raintree Library, 2015.

Simons, Lisa M. Bolt. *Transportation Long Ago and Today*. Long Ago and Today. North Mankato, MN: Capstone Press, 2015.

Internet Sites

Arthur's Family History Fun! Game
https://pbskids.org/arthur/games/family-history-fun#/

Family History Guide: Kids Corner
https://www.thefhguide.com/act-children.html

Family Tree Printable
http://www.growinglittleleaves.com/uploads/7/8/0/4/7804837/birds_on_wire_family_tree.pdf

Critical Thinking Questions

1. How many people are in your family?

2. How do you keep in touch with friends and family that do not live close to you?

3. What chores do you do to help your family?

Index